# Eternal Musings

Amrita  Lamba

Presentation by *BookLeaf Publishing*

Web: www.bookleafpub.com

E-mail: info@bookleafpub.com


ISBN: 9789357619288

First edition 2023

# Night Spell

I wandered mischievously,
Through the woods,
Along with the bashful moon,
Verily happily veiled by the clouds.
The woods and clouds,
And the moon and I,
Together metamorphosed,
The rich purple plum coloured hour,
Into a night spell.

# Perceptions

They dawn.
Quiet, woolly and clamorous cries
bring a cascading,
deafening clarity.
Reasons and emotions connive
in weaving a congruence in acuity.
The taste of pure water.
The moon's reflection in twinkling eyes.
Invictus.
But, what if?
The veil drops.
The spell is broken.
A hologram stares.
And something even beyond?
Who knows?
Illogic,
Imbecile perspicacity,
Undergird hydra-headed perceptions.
The world is not flat, after all.

# Trickster

"Lies," said a wise man,
"Is truth in disguise;
"I've often seen the two,
"Woven together,
"Indistinguishable,
"The same."
"Truth," said a wise man,
"Is lies laid bare;
"I've often see the two,
"Separate,
"Distinguishable,
"Different."
And I believed both the wise men;
For lies is for me
Truth in disguise,
And truth is,
Lies laid bare.
But I've never seen these,
As such.

# On Love

I waited and waited
but you scarcely showed,
I somehow felt there must be love
but how was it I didn't know?
A butcher vehemently and ceaselessly slaying,
With merciless candour and drunken dreaminess.
And still appear upright and pious,
Inculpating me for crime?
Unsteady and floating,
I oscillated between fading joy and lasting pain,
With a longing to escape everything and
simultaneously to be found.
And just like that the world became magical again
and lost lacklustre all the same.
To be ripped apart and then strung together,
To be destroyed and saved all at once,
Are love's greatest tribulations?
And you remain unconcerned, aloof, unaware or
whatever.
Alone I wander in this quest.
Perhaps they rightly say,
Narrow is the path of love
for there is no room for two here.
You are your own soulmate.

# Melancholy

I never sought you.
But you found your way
and became my companion.
I never felt you.
But you glided over
and overlay my being.
I never saw you.
But you scorned at my oversight
and became visual.
I never tasted you.
But you savoured this ignorance
and created an unknown appetite.
I never heard you.
But you droned
and ripened a humdrum.
I never knew you.
But now I remember you.
Unawares.

# The Regimen

A ferret, a unicorn, a wombat,
a dumbo octopus, a python, a kangaroo, and a
slug,
Were subjects of a tiger's kingdom,
Appositely known as The Regimen.
A gaze vacant and stony as the sun,
Vied to drill discipline into the
subjects' secret escapes even,
The tiger
was pitiless.
The subjects could not hear one another.
Their abilities wrecked
by gyrating decorum.
No sugar, no chocolate.
Only bite sized steamed fare.
Zesty watermelon fries
and raw fit cookie bars,
Found place in fancies.
For imagination could not be colonised
by the tiger's command-dimmed tide.
Then one day,
Came a lion to the kingdom.
Diligence confronted laziness,
And set afloat a mutiny.
Yet the tide remain unchanged.

The tiger still reigns.
The subjects reined in.
They don't hear one another.
But they dream,
For dreams come true they say.

# An ode to the Self

O fiery burning sun,
How are you suffused with ambrosial nectar
without it being scorched?
Your formless form deludes me,
Stern yet loving,
Innocent and a trickster,
All at once.
How may I feel purity?
Words elude me,
Reality and illusion
are elided into eternity,
You remain an enigma
for me.

# The Deluded One

A melodious hum,
Entrancing all, including the
hardened
within its fold.
Soft butter,
Inflaming and evoking
gluttony,
Among the starved
and sated alike.
Blissful Being,
Elegantly gliding
With aplomb,
A swan.

# On Not Knowing

Sound unheard.
Neither sugar, spice, brine, sour, bitter,
pungent, astringent nor umami.
Form and formless, useless binary.
Blank.
Desperate for a volte-face.
To know.

# Dilemma

The struggling notes barely escape,
Over the floodgates of the musical cauldron,
With fleeting yet recurring fervour,
A veiled chameleon,
Staying as traces of grey,
The ultimate trickster.

# Consciousness

I see the glistening spider webs, the shimmering
trees in the moonlight,
I watch the tiniest to the largest nocturnal
creatures,
But nobody sees me.

I feel and sense all nocturnal activity,
Yet remain detached and unconditioned,
But no one is aware or feels my presence,
I am in the wind, the whisper, and the silence of
the night,
I am in the unforgiving storm that destroys,
Yet no one even doubtingly ascribes these forms
to me?

I wait, patiently and impatiently, without
expectations,
For something or someone to perceive me,
I dance and sing and scream and stay silent,
And no one hears or sees me.

# Fearlessness

13

As the bells slowly cease to ring,
The fragrance of sandalwood surfaces,
And touches my heart like a soft feather,
It feels like a peeling and a return into my
original skin,
That raw, unfettered self.

# Peace

14

From the deeply penetrating silence,
The smell of burning camphor,
Cuts through the dark space,
And appears as still water,
Reflecting the lustrous moon's contours.

# The Despot

15

The overbearing bell's chime,
A deafening silence,
Tasteless in the mouth, and in spirit,
A delinquent, martinet demeanour,
Sweet orange or an impostor?
Ever stumbled into quicksand
and found the ground beneath slip away?
Trapped?
That's how it feels,
Sans rights, sans thoughts, sans everything,
Only stark obedience reigns

# In Pursuit to Be

Silence interrupted,
Insatiability,
Holding a bubble,
Seeing a real pantomime?
Blurred homecoming,
An elusive quest,
Wrestled, hoodwinked,
Graced, secured,
Empty and free,
A paradoxical harmony
to Be.

# Pattern

The ticking of a pendulum clock,
Different coloured sweet gems
tasting the same.
The ebb and flow of waves,
Yellow is always lemon,
Expectations met, expectedly.
A vacuous smile,
A merry-go-round,
A grudging surrender,
Make uncertainty
delectable.

# The urge (for excellence)

The rosy wine
blushed,
Deeply satisfied,
Silent,
Frangipani essence
everywhere.

# Alchemy

Silently you become
ephemeral again.
Cud-chewing.
Retroductive.
Abstracting and concretising
back and forth.
Basic instincts
like these
drive the Universe,
till silently you become
ephemeral, yet again.

www.ingramcontent.com/pod-product-compliance
Lightning Source LLC
Chambersburg PA
CBHW070729160726
48003CB00006BA/2420